Akiko and Amy Part 2

I Talk You Talk Press

CONTENTS

INTRODUCTION

This is Part 2 of Akiko and Amy's Story. The story starts in the graded reader *Akiko and Amy Part 1*.

1. AMY AND DICK

Akiko had only met Dick, Amy's husband, once. But Akiko knew a lot about Dick. Amy told Akiko that Dick's hometown, Spurton, is very small. It's in Montana, in the United States. Dick's father is called Jacob. He owns a gas station. It's the only gas station in the town. Jacob is the postman too. He drives a small truck around town. He delivers newspapers, letters and parcels. Jacob also takes shopping and mail to people who live on farms outside the town.

The gas station does not have any staff. When Dick's father is working as the postman, there is no one to serve gasoline or fix cars. People have to wait until Dick's father comes back. Akiko thought that was very strange. "Don't people get angry?" she asked.

Amy laughed. "Maybe people get angry. But if they don't want to wait, they have to drive fifty miles to the next gas station."

"How far is fifty miles?" asked Akiko.

"About eighty kilometres," answered Amy.

Dick's mother died when he was eleven. He has no brothers or sisters. He left Spurton when he was twelve and he went to live in Butte with his aunt. He went to junior high school and high school in Butte, and then he went to university in San Francisco. Dick has been back to Spurton for vacations, but he has not lived in his hometown since he was twelve.

Amy and Dick met at university. Amy's home city is Boston.

Akiko and Amy had a plan to go shopping on Tuesday. But on Tuesday morning, Amy called Akiko. "I can't go shopping today," she said. "I am taking Dick to the airport. He is going home to

Montana. His father had an accident."

"Oh, no!" said Akiko. "I hope he is OK."

"So do I," answered Amy. "Dick will call me or Skype me the day after tomorrow. Then I will know more."

"Please tell Dick I am very sorry," said Akiko. "I hope everything will be OK."

"I will. Now I must go, or Dick will be late for his flight."

On Thursday, Amy went to Akiko's apartment for coffee. Amy looked tired and worried.

"Is Jacob OK?" asked Akiko.

"His eyes were damaged. He can't see well."

"Will his eyes get better?" asked Akiko.

"Maybe yes. Maybe no. If he can't see well, he can't drive. He can't work in his gas station," explained Amy.

"What will he do?"

"He wants Dick to go home. He wants to give Dick the postman's job and the gas station."

"Oh!" cried Akiko. *If Dick and Amy go back to the USA, I won't be able to meet Amy,* she thought. *I'll lose my friend.* Then she thought, *I am not a nice person. I am thinking only about myself. I should think about Jacob, Dick and Amy.*

"Will you be happy in that small town?" Akiko asked Amy.

"Oh, Akiko! I grew up in Boston. I like shops and movies and restaurants and big cities. Dick likes fishing and hiking and horse riding. He could be happy in the country. But Dick doesn't want to go back to Spurton now. Dick likes his life here. He enjoys teaching English at the university, meeting new people and travelling."

"So you won't go back to the USA?" said Akiko.

"If Jacob's eyes don't get better, I think we will go. Dick must help his father," said Amy.

"What will you do?" asked Akiko.

"I don't know, but I will find something to do. Do you think I could open a Japanese restaurant? Or maybe I could get a job as a teacher. There is an elementary school in the town. I have been to Spurton a few times. Dick and I went there for Christmas and Thanksgiving. I thought the people there were very nice."

Akiko thought Amy was very strong. Akiko was sure that Amy did not want to live in such as small town. She knew that Amy was a city girl.

Dick stayed in America for two weeks. Then he returned to Japan. His father was still in hospital, but Dick had missed many classes at the university. He had to catch up and teach extra classes. He was very busy. Amy said she didn't know what would happen. If Dick wanted to go to Montana, she would go with him.

One day, about three weeks later, Amy called Akiko. "Are you free today? I want to take you to a nice restaurant. I want to buy you lunch."

Amy and Akiko went to a very nice French restaurant. Amy was smiling. She was very happy.

"I have some good news," she said. "Jacob's eyes are better. They are not perfect, but he can drive."

"That's great news!" cried Akiko. "I'm so happy for him."

"I have more news," said Amy. "Jacob met a nurse in the hospital. She is the same age as him. She grew up near Spurton. They even went to the same elementary school. Her husband died ten years ago. Jacob and the nurse have decided to get married!"

"That's wonderful," said Akiko. "Will you go to the wedding?"

"No," said Amy. "But they will come to Japan for their honeymoon."

2. DINNER PARTIES

Akiko and Amy have been friends for six months. They meet two or three times a week.

Amy often says to Akiko, "Come to my apartment for dinner. My husband wants to meet you and your husband."

Akiko always makes an excuse. She always says, "My husband is very busy right now." Or, "I think my husband wants to meet his friend this week. Anyway, I have met your husband."

Amy always laughs. "You only met once, for a very short time!"

Amy does not understand why Akiko and her husband don't want to come to her apartment for dinner.

One day, Amy asked Akiko. "You and your husband don't want to come to our apartment for dinner. Why don't you want to come?"

Akiko's face turned red. "I want to come, but Seiji doesn't want to," she said quietly.

"Why not?" asked Amy.

Akiko looked at the floor. "My husband can read English a little. But he doesn't speak English."

"But, Akiko! Dick speaks very good Japanese! He can speak to Seiji in Japanese!" said Amy.

Akiko was surprised. "When Dick spoke to me, he spoke in English!"

"Yes. He spoke in English because he knows you want to practice English!" said Amy.

"Oh," said Akiko.

That night Akiko told her husband. "Dick, Amy's husband, speaks very good Japanese. He wants to meet you. Please can we go to their apartment for dinner?"

Seiji thought about it. He wasn't sure.

"If we go to their house for dinner, we will have to ask them to come here for dinner."

"Yes," answered Akiko. "That's OK."

"But our apartment is very small."

"Our apartment is the same size as their apartment!"

"We don't know what they can eat."

"They eat everything. They like Japanese food."

"We don't have a table for four people."

"We can sit on the floor."

"American people do not sit on the floor," said Seiji. "I know that."

Akiko was getting angry. "They live in Japan. They can eat Japanese food. I am sure they can sit on the floor."

"Do we have enough knives and forks?"

"Seiji! Yes, we do! Anyway, they can use chopsticks very well! Many American people use chopsticks when they eat in Japanese and Chinese restaurants. It is no problem."

Seiji was worried. He was very shy, and he was worried about his English. But he knew Akiko wanted to go to Dick and Amy's for dinner. So he said, "OK, let's go".

Seiji practiced English all week. Every day at lunchtime, he learned some new words. One of the men in his office was very good at English. His name was Wada. Wada san went to English classes at night. He was very proud of his English. He often talked about his English teacher, who was an American. Seiji wanted to ask Wada san to tell him some good English words. But Seiji thought Wada san would laugh at him, because Seiji's English was so bad.

The night of the dinner party Seiji was nervous. Akiko was very happy. She was not nervous. Akiko rang the doorbell of the apartment. Dick answered the door. "Irasshai! Welcome! Come in!"

Suddenly Seiji felt very good. The American was very nice. He spoke Japanese well. There was a delicious smell of beef cooking. Seiji loved beef.

The dinner party was very good. The food was delicious. Dick and Seiji talked about baseball and soccer. Amy and Akiko talked about food and fashion. Seiji was amazed. Akiko could speak English very well. She spoke quickly and she was very relaxed.

The next day, Seiji went to work. He saw Wada san. "I went out for coffee with my American teacher last night," said Wada san. "He says my English is getting very good."

"That's nice, Wada san," said Seiji. "I know you work very hard. It's good to speak English. I must practice my English. I have an American friend. I would like to speak to him in English."

"You?!" Wada san was amazed. "You have an American friend?!"

"Oh, yes," said Seiji. Seiji felt good.

A month later, Akiko told Seiji that she had invited Dick and Amy for dinner on Saturday.

Suddenly Seiji was nervous again. "I don't think it's a good idea."

"Of course it's a good idea!" said Akiko. "It's the night of your birthday. We will have a small party, just four people. It will be fun."

"What will they eat?" asked Seiji.

"It's your birthday, so I will cook your favourite food. I'm sure they will like it!"

Seiji was worried. He started practicing English again. He bought a lot of wine and beer and whisky.

Akiko said he was crazy. "We don't need so much alcohol! They only drink a little!"

On Seiji's birthday, Akiko was busy. She cooked Seiji's favourite food - seafood and rice.

Amy and Dick brought birthday presents for Seiji.

Amy had made a birthday cake. On the top of the cake were the words *o-tanjobi omedeto*! (This means 'happy birthday' in Japanese.) Dick gave Seiji a Seattle Mariners baseball team cap. Seiji was very happy.

Dick and Seiji drank some whisky.

Dick said, "I like to drink whisky, but not every day. Whisky is good for a special day."

Seiji had a great birthday party.

On Monday, Seiji saw Wada san in the office car park.

"Wada san! Look! I have a Seattle Mariners baseball cap!" he said.

"Oh, I have one too," said Wada san. "Where did you get it?"

"Well, I have an American friend. His name is Dick. He gave it to me."

"Do you speak to Dick in English?" asked Wada san.

"No, I don't. Dick speaks very good Japanese," said Seiji.

"You should practice speaking to him in English," said Wada san.

Seiji thought that was a good idea. Next time he met Dick, he would try and speak in English!

3. HONEYMOONS

Akiko and Amy were friends for more than six months before their husbands met. Now Dick and Seiji are good friends too. If Seiji gets home by 6:00pm, on a Friday night, the four friends go out to eat together. They like to go to a sushi restaurant in the centre of the city.

One Friday in August, they were eating sushi together. They were talking about Dick's father, Jacob. In May, Jacob had an accident and damaged his eyes. Dick thought he should go back to America to look after his father, and to take over his father's business. Then there were two lucky events. Jacob's eyes got better. His eyes are not perfect, but he can do most things. The second lucky event was that Jacob met a nurse in the hospital. When they were children, they went to the same elementary school. Her name is Maria. Now Jacob and Maria are planning to get married. They will come to Japan for their honeymoon.

"Will Jacob and Maria stay with you?" asked Seiji.

"Yes. We will give them our bedroom and we will sleep in the living room," said Amy.

"Oh. Can they sleep on futon?" asked Seiji.

"Maybe," answered Dick. "But Amy and I bought a bed. The shop will deliver the bed tomorrow. So my father and his new wife can use it while they are staying with us."

"Are you happy, Dick?" asked Akiko. "Have you met Maria yet?"

"No, I haven't met her yet. I remember my own mother very well," said Dick. "I was eleven when she died. But my father has been alone for a long time. I think he is very happy now. If Maria makes my father happy, then I will be very pleased!"

"We have made many plans," said Amy. "We are going to take them sightseeing in this area, and on two trips. We will go to Hiroshima for a weekend, and to Kyoto for three days."

"Don't forget, they are going to come to our apartment for dinner," said Akiko. "Please leave a free evening for that!"

"Maria and Dad are going to have a full schedule," said Dick. "I hope they won't get too tired. It's their honeymoon. I hope they can relax."

"Japanese people often go sightseeing on their honeymoons," said Seiji. "I guess they get tired too."

"Where did you go on your honeymoon?" asked Amy.

"We haven't had our honeymoon yet," Akiko said. "We are planning it. Maybe next spring we will go on our honeymoon. Where did you go for your honeymoon?"

"We didn't have one," said Amy. "Dick was finishing his university study and we didn't have any money. Sometime we will take a wonderful trip. We will call that our honeymoon."

"Maybe in two years. It will be our five-year anniversary. We'll go somewhere very romantic," added Dick.

"Yes! Bali or Phuket or the Maldives!" smiled Amy. "Where would you and Seiji like to go?"

"Oh, Europe of course! We want to go to Paris, Rome, Venice and Berlin. It will be wonderful!" answered Akiko.

"Aaah," said Dick. "A sightseeing honeymoon."

"Well, Akiko and I want to see Europe. In my office it is very difficult to take time off for a vacation, but time off for a honeymoon is OK. So we will take a sightseeing vacation and call it a honeymoon. I think we can go for ten days!" said Seiji.

"What about the romance?" asked Amy, laughing.

"Well, once every few months, Seiji and I go to a hot spring resort in the mountains. We usually stay one night," said Akiko. "It is very quiet and beautiful! That's our romance! You will have to arrange some romance for Jacob and Maria when they come. What will you do?"

"I don't know yet. Maybe a hot spring resort trip is a good idea," said Dick.

"Yes, I think they will enjoy that," said Seiji. "We could all go together!"

"That's a great idea!" said Dick. "Let's do that!"

"Yes, let's!" said everyone.

Amy and Akiko smiled at each other. Their husbands had become very good friends!

4. AMY'S MOTHER

Amy and Akiko went for a bicycle ride. They rode along the road next to the lake. The weather was beautiful. After an hour, they stopped at a café for coffee.

"I have some news," said Amy. "My mother is coming to stay."

Akiko was very interested. "Your mother is coming from Boston?"

"No. My parents are divorced. My mother lives in San Francisco now. She has a business trip to Seoul. So she will take a vacation and come here when her business is finished."

"How long will she stay?" asked Akiko.

"Only three days. She is always very busy."

"Will you give her your bedroom? Or will she sleep in the living room?" asked Akiko.

"Oh. She won't stay in our apartment. She will stay in a hotel. I will reserve a room for her at Supreme Towers."

"Wow. That's expensive!" said Amy.

"I know. But my mother would not be happy with a normal hotel."

"Why won't she stay with you?" Akiko asked.

"Well. Our apartment is too small. There is only one bathroom. It would be a bad idea. Also, I love my mother, but I can't live with her."

"You can't live with your mother?"

"Wait and see," said Amy. "You will understand when you meet her."

Two weeks later, Amy's mother came to visit. She invited Akiko to join her and Amy for lunch at the Supreme Towers Hotel.

Akiko wore a smart dress and a white jacket. The Supreme Towers Hotel was very expensive. Amy met Akiko at the front desk of the hotel. Akiko was very surprised. Amy was wearing jeans and an old sweater.

"Oh, my clothes are wrong!" said Akiko.

"No!" said Amy. "Your clothes are perfect! My mother will love you."

Amy's mother was waiting for them in a table in the restaurant. She jumped up and kissed Akiko.

"It's so nice to meet you! Thank you for coming! Amy has told me so much about you! Look at you! You are so pretty! So cute!!"

Amy's mother was talking very loudly. Akiko didn't know what to do or what to say. Everyone in the restaurant was looking at them.

Akiko sat down quickly. "Call me Linda," said Amy's mother.

"Err…nice to meet you Linda," said Akiko. She was nervous.

Amy's mother looked amazing. She looked about 30 or 35 years old. She was blonde. Her make-up was perfect. She was wearing a white suit and very high-heeled shoes.

Akiko could not believe she was Amy's mother. She looked so young.

The lunch was delicious. Linda talked and talked and talked. She loved Japan. She loved Japanese culture and Japanese food. She said Japanese women were so beautiful. Akiko was happy that Linda liked Japan, but she couldn't say anything because Linda did not stop talking!

Then Amy said, "Mom! Be quiet! You are making Akiko nervous."

"Oh no!" said Linda. "I'm so sorry. Amy always says I talk too much."

Akiko had never met anyone like Linda before. She was so friendly and nice. She was very glamorous but she made Akiko feel shy.

When lunch was finished, Akiko said, "I have brought you a very small present. I hope you like it."

Linda opened her present.

Linda smiled. "Japanese plates! I love them! You are so sweet! Thank you Akiko! You are a good friend for Amy, so I brought you a present too!"

She took a big box out of her white and gold bag. She gave it to Akiko.

Akiko didn't want to open the present in a restaurant but Linda asked her to. "Open it! Open it!"

It was a Louis Vuitton bag. Akiko could not believe it.

"Thank you!" she said. "But it is too expensive!"

"No," said Linda. "I read in a flight magazine that Louis Vuitton bags are very popular in Japan."

Akiko did not know what to say. "I like it very much, thank you."

"That's good," said Linda. "Now, tomorrow I am going to hire a car and driver. I want to go sightseeing with Amy. I hope you will come with us, Akiko. You can be our interpreter and guide."

Amy and Akiko went back to the apartment building together.

"Now you understand why I can't live with my mother," said Amy.

"Yes. I think your mother is wonderful. But I do understand. She talks a lot!"

"Do you like the bag?" asked Amy.

"Yes, I like it very much, but I am embarrassed. Louis Vuitton bags are very expensive."

"Oh, my mother has a lot of money. Don't worry," said Amy

"If my mother-in-law sees it, I will have to say it is a copy!" Akiko laughed.

Amy and Akiko climbed up the stairs.

"This is a quiet building," said Amy. "If my mother stayed here, she would be too noisy. The neighbours would complain!"

5. A DIFFICULT QUESTION

Amy's mother Linda was visiting. She wasn't staying in Amy and Dick's apartment. She was staying in an expensive hotel. Today the plan was to go sightseeing. Linda had hired a car and a driver. She asked Akiko to go with her and Amy. Amy and Akiko planned to meet Linda at her hotel at 9:30.

At 8:30 Akiko got a call on her mobile phone. It was Amy.

"Akiko. I'm sorry. I can't go sightseeing today. A man from the company that will publish my book contacted me. He is in Japan for only three days and he asked me to meet him in Tokyo. I have to take a flight at 10:30 to get there in time."

Akiko was disappointed, but she knew that this was good news for Amy. "That's exciting," she said. "You have finished your book and you will be a famous writer!"

"Oh, no," laughed Amy. "It's not that kind of book! It's a pity I have to go today. Please go sightseeing with my mother."

"I can't!" said Akiko. "My English is not good."

"Your English is great! Please go with her."

Akiko was very nervous. Linda was very nice and friendly, but she talked a lot. She made Akiko feel shy. But then Akiko thought, *Amy is my good friend. I should help her. Linda is very kind. She gave me a Louis Vuitton bag. I am nervous, but I must do this.*

"OK. I will try," she said. "But please call your mother and explain. Please tell her you can't go."

Akiko went to the hotel. She took her new bag. It made her feel good.

15

Linda was waiting next to the front desk. "Good morning, Akiko. I am sorry Amy can't come, but we will have a good day."

The car was very big and very comfortable. Linda and Akiko sat in the back. Linda talked a lot. She enjoyed the scenery. They went to a temple and a shrine. Akiko tried to explain everything. When she couldn't explain well, the driver helped her. He spoke very good English. After a little while, Akiko felt more relaxed.

At lunchtime, Akiko and Linda went to a traditional noodle restaurant.

"Please order for me," said Linda.

"Can you eat with chopsticks?" Akiko asked.

Linda laughed. "Of course! I live in San Francisco. There are many Chinese restaurants there. I love Chinese food."

"I hope you will like this Japanese food," said Akiko.

Akiko ordered lunch sets. Linda was very interested in the food. She asked many questions. Akiko explained about the miso soup and the buckwheat noodles.

After lunch, Linda asked Akiko to order more tea. "I love this restaurant and this food and the tea. Let's sit and relax for a while."

While they were drinking the tea, Linda asked Akiko, "What do you do?"

Akiko didn't understand. "What do I do? Sorry, I don't know what that means."

"What do you do means 'what is your job'?" Linda explained.

"Oh. I don't have a job," Akiko answered.

"You are so pretty and so clever. You don't have any children. Don't you get bored?" asked Linda.

"Sometimes," answered Akiko. "I studied to be a chef. But then I got married and came to this small city. I used to be bored, and sometimes I was unhappy. Then I met Amy. It was very good for me. My life is interesting now."

"Of course you have a Japanese husband," said Linda. "Maybe your husband doesn't want you to have a job."

"Oh, no!" Akiko wanted to explain. "My husband is very nice. If I wanted to have a job, he would never say no. My mother-in-law would be very angry, but my husband would say it was OK. There is a problem. There are not many jobs for chefs in a small city like this, and I have no experience. I got married as soon as I finished studying. Also chefs work at night and on Saturdays and Sundays. I would not

16

see my husband very much. I wouldn't like that."

"Oh, I understand," said Linda. "It's good for Amy to have you as a friend."

"It's good for me too," said Akiko.

Akiko told Linda that she was happy. But that night, she sat in her apartment and thought about her life. Amy wrote books. She was a writer. Akiko didn't do anything. *Would I like to have a job?* Akiko wondered. She cooked and cleaned every day. Two or three times a week she and Amy spent time together. *Would it be nice to be like Amy and earn money?*

6. A WONDERFUL INVITATION

Akiko has a computer. She often surfs the Internet and she has an email account. She doesn't use her email account very much. Her husband Seiji calls her, and her best friend Amy either calls her, or sends a text message to her mobile phone. Akiko checks her emails every day, but usually there is only junk mail.

Then one day, there was an email from Linda, Amy's mother! The email was sent to both Amy and Akiko.

--- *Hi Girls!*

I have a nice surprise for you. My great friend Homer is a movie producer. He has just made a movie about a young doctor from Osaka, who falls in love with an American student. Some of the movie takes place in America, and some in Japan. The premiere of the movie is in Osaka next Saturday, and Homer has given me tickets for you and your husbands!

Homer has invited all of you to the gala party after the movie too. The party is at the Ritz-Carlton. I am sending you the tickets by courier. And I am giving you a little Christmas present. I have bought air tickets for you all to fly to Osaka and I have made reservations for you at the Ritz-Carlton so you can stay there after the party.

Have a great time!

Love, Linda.---

Akiko stared at the computer screen. She could not believe it! Then another email came from Linda. This message was only sent to Akiko.

--- Dear Akiko, The party will be very glamorous. Please make sure that Amy wears something nice! Love, Linda---

Akiko laughed. Linda has beautiful clothes and is very fashionable. Amy likes to wear jeans and sweaters, and she almost never wears make up.

The doorbell of Akiko's apartment rang. It was Amy.

"Come in!" said Akiko. "I got Linda's email. It's so exciting!"

Amy came in and sat on the floor. "Yes, it is exciting. But Dick won't be able to go with me. He is taking some of his students to an English camp next weekend."

"Oh," said Akiko. "That's too bad. But you will go?"

"Yes, I'll go," Amy smiled. "I think Homer is my mother's new boyfriend. I want to go so I can see what he is like!"

When Seiji came home from work, Akiko told him all about the wonderful invitation. "But we can't go," said Seiji.

"What?" cried Akiko. "Why not?"

"I have to work. It's the end of the month. I always work on Saturdays at the end of the month."

"But I could go!" said Akiko. "Dick can't go either, but Amy will go without him."

Seiji wasn't so sure. He didn't like the idea. He didn't think that his wife should go to a gala party in Osaka without him.

"I'll think about it," said Seiji. "I don't think my mother would like it."

"I don't care what your mother thinks!" shouted Akiko. She went into the bedroom and closed the door very loudly.

Seiji was tired. He didn't know what to do. Akiko wanted to go to Osaka very much but he didn't want Akiko to go without him. He looked in the cupboard and found a bottle of whisky. Then he took the bottle of whisky and went to Amy and Dick's apartment. He rang the doorbell. Amy came to the door.

"Can I talk with Dick please?" asked Seiji. "I need some advice."

About an hour later, Seiji went back to his apartment. It was very quiet. Akiko was still in the bedroom. He went to the door and called out.

"Akiko. I'm sorry. Of course you should go to Osaka. You will be with Amy, and you can share a hotel room. I was silly. I didn't think.

I was jealous."

Akiko ran out and hugged her husband. "I wish you could come too. It won't be the same without you. But I want to go very much. Is it OK?"

"Of course it's OK. I hope you and Amy have a wonderful time."

The next morning, after Dick and Seiji had left for work, Amy and Akiko sat down to plan their trip to Osaka.

"What are you going to wear to the party?" Akiko asked Amy.

"Oh, anything," answered Amy.

"But it will be a very formal party. We have to dress well," said Akiko. "I don't know what to wear."

"Well I don't have any formal dresses," said Amy. "And Dick and I are saving money for a trip. I can't buy a formal dress. It would be too expensive."

"I don't have anything to wear either," said Akiko. "But I have an idea. There is a used clothes shop near the city library. We should go and look there."

"Do you think they would have anything to fit me?" asked Amy. "Japanese women are much shorter than I am."

Amy is very slim, but she is very tall.

"That's true," said Akiko. "But very short dresses are in fashion now. If we can find something from a few years ago, when longer dresses were in fashion, I think it will be OK."

The trip to the clothes shop was very successful. Amy found a black cocktail dress that fitted perfectly. Akiko bought a very cute red dress. She looked very good in it. They also bought a black jacket for Amy. It was autumn. They thought it would be warm in the party, but it would be cold outside.

They took their shopping back to the apartments. "Now we are ready!" smiled Akiko. "I can't wait for next Saturday!"

7. THE PARTY

Amy and Akiko took the plane to Osaka on Saturday morning. Dick was away with his students, and Seiji was busy at work. So Amy drove her car to the airport and left it in the car park. Akiko was so excited she talked all the time.

Amy thought this was very funny. "Calm down!" she said. "You are usually very quiet. Today you're like a crazy person!"

"I'm sorry," said Akiko. "Nothing like this has ever happened to me before. I feel like a film star. Your mother is so kind! I want to tell everyone that I am going to a movie premiere, and to a party at the Ritz-Carlton!"

They arrived at the hotel at lunchtime. Amy ordered sandwiches and coffee from room service. They spent the afternoon getting dressed, doing each other's hair and putting on makeup.

"I feel silly," said Amy. "I almost never wear make-up."

"You look great!" said Akiko. "Everyone will be looking at you. They will ask, 'Is that one of the stars from the movie?'"

Most of the guests for the premiere were staying at the same hotel. The film company had arranged limousines to take everyone to the theatre for the movie premiere. Akiko and Amy were not important guests, so their limousine left early. The premiere was at 7:00pm, but they had to leave the hotel at 6:00pm.

Akiko thought this was a good thing. "We will be able to watch all the stars coming into the theatre! I can't wait!"

When Amy and Akiko got out of the limousine at the theatre, there were already some fans standing outside the theatre. People

21

clapped and took photographs.

"I wonder who they think we are?" laughed Amy.

"Oh, movie stars!" Akiko replied.

They waited inside the lobby of the movie theatre and watched the movie stars enter. Their dresses were not as amazing as those that stars wear to the Academy Awards in the United States, but they were very beautiful. Amy and Akiko enjoyed the movie. It was a very romantic story. After the movie, there were limousines waiting to take them back to the hotel for the party.

The party was fun. Akiko was too shy to talk to people, but she enjoyed watching the guests. Amy was not so shy but she said, "These people are so different from us! I don't know what to say to them. I tell them I enjoyed the movie. I say that I think it will be a great success. Then I ask the non-Japanese people if they are enjoying Japan. I can't think of any other conversation."

Linda's friend Homer came to speak to them. "I hope you enjoyed the movie," he said.

"Oh, yes! It was wonderful," answered Akiko.

"We're enjoying the party too," said Amy. "Thank you for inviting us."

"I hope you and I will be good friends," Homer said to Amy. "I hope you will come to the States for our big event. I want it to be a family affair."

"A family affair?" asked Amy.

"Well, yes. Didn't Linda tell you? We're planning to get married soon."

"Oh, congratulations! I guess my mother wanted it to be a surprise. Dick and I will certainly come to the wedding."

"Bring your lovely friend and her husband too! I must go and talk to some more people. Enjoy yourselves!" Homer went away.

Akiko was worried. *Amy must be upset that her mother didn't tell her about her marriage plans,* she thought. Akiko looked at Amy. She was laughing. "My mother! She's unbelievable!"

The next day Amy and Akiko were on their way back home. On the plane, Amy took a diary from her bag and started writing in it.

"What are you writing?" asked Akiko.

"My plan for next week," answered Amy. "I have a lot to do. The publisher wants me to make some changes to the textbook I wrote, and they want teachers' notes too. Then Dick is planning a trip to the

USA for his students. I promised Dick I would help him with his plans. He wants me to go with him and the students. So, I'm making a list of everything I have to do."

"You are so busy!" said Akiko.

Amy smiled and wrote some more.

Akiko looked out the window of the plane. It had been a wonderful experience. She had enjoyed Osaka, the movie premiere and the party very much. Now she was going home. She would be very pleased to see Seiji of course, but then tomorrow he would go to work.

Everyone was busy. Everyone had plans and things to do.

I don't have anything, thought Akiko. *My days are always the same. If Amy is busy, maybe we can't go out together. My life is so boring! I must do something to change it!*

THANK YOU

Thank you for reading Akiko and Amy Part 2. (Word count: 5,907)
We hope you enjoyed it. Akiko and Amy's story continues in part 3.

If you would like to read more graded readers, please visit our
website http://www.italkyoutalk.com

Other Level 3 graded readers include
A Dangerous Weekend
A Holiday to Remember
Akiko and Amy Part 1
Akiko and Amy Part 3
Be My Valentine
Different Seas
Enjoy Your Business Trip
Enjoy Your Homestay
I Need a Friend
Old Jack's Ghost Stories from England (1)
Old Jack's Ghost Stories from England (2)
Old Jack's Ghost Stories from Ireland
Old Jack's Ghost Stories from Japan
Old Jack's Ghost Stories from Scotland
Old Jack's Ghost Stories from Wales
Party Time!
Stories for Christmas
The Curse

Together Again
Who is Holly?

ABOUT THE AUTHOR

I Talk You Talk Press is a Japan-based publisher of language textbooks, graded readers and language learning/teaching resources.

Our team is made up of highly experienced language teachers and translators, who have all studied at least one additional language to an advanced level.

This experience enables us to design our materials from the perspective of both the teacher and the learner. We consult with both teachers and language learners when designing our textbooks and graded readers, and test our materials extensively in the classroom before publication.

We are a fast-growing press, and currently publish graded readers for learners of English. We publish new graded readers monthly.